HARRY KANE

EMILY HIBBS

FOOTBALL LEGENDS

HARRY KANE

SCHOLASTIC

Published in the UK by Scholastic Children's Books, 2020
Euston House, 24 Eversholt Street, London, NW1 1DB
A division of Scholastic Limited

London – New York – Toronto – Sydney – Auckland
Mexico City – New Delhi – Hong Kong

SCHOLASTIC and associated logos are trademarks and/or
registered trademarks of Scholastic Inc.

Text © Emily Hibbs, 2020
Cover illustration © Stanley Chow, 2020

ISBN 978 14071 9843 9

A CIP catalogue record for this book is available from the British Library.

Printed by CPI Group (UK) Ltd, Croydon, CR0 4YY
Papers used by Scholastic Children's Books are made from
wood grown in sustainable forests.

1 3 5 7 9 10 8 6 4 2

www.scholastic.co.uk

Contents

ENGLAND'S HERO

On the evening of 3 July 2018, England's youngest ever World Cup captain stepped up to the penalty spot in Spartak Stadium, Moscow. The match against Colombia had come down to a penalty shootout – something every England fan had been dreading, given the country's terrible track record. But there was always hope that this team could make history, especially with superstar striker Harry Kane as their captain. Harry had already scored six goals in the tournament, including one earlier on in the Colombia match. He was on his way to winning the World Cup Golden Boot and – if he could just hold his nerve – heading to England's first semi-final in twenty-eight years.

But just a few seasons before, none of this would have seemed very likely at all. It had taken a lot of hard work and self-belief for Harry Kane to get to this moment.

Harry had loved football for as long as he could remember. He started playing for his local side when he was six years old. Like his family, Harry was a massive Tottenham Hotspur fan, but spent several years with other clubs before he made it into the Spurs Under-13s side.

Not fast enough, not athletic enough, not strong enough, not big enough – Harry would hear it all. Even when he finally signed his first professional contract, he faced months as a substitute on the bench, itching to be given a chance to play. Shipped off on four loan spells to other clubs – during two of which he barely managed to get on the pitch – he was hardly a likely choice for a future England captain. But Harry's passion and dedication carried him through the hard times, and he kept fighting to prove he deserved a place on Tottenham Hotspur's first team.

Finally, a breakthrough season for Spurs made the world sit up and pay attention. From then on in, it was goals, goals, goals. By the time he arrived at the 2018 World Cup finals, Harry had over one hundred Premier League goals and two Premier League Golden Boots under his belt. But he wasn't finished yet.

As Harry eyed up the goal in that all-important penalty shootout against Colombia, he wasn't thinking of any of those triumphs or heartbreaks, setbacks or successes – he was thinking only of how to get the ball into the back of the net, like he had so many times before. Harry ran through his usual penalty routine, took a short run-up, and blasted the ball straight into the bottom corner. Colombia's goalkeeper didn't stand a chance. Harry was pleased – but it wasn't over yet. This wasn't just about him, after all. When England's final penalty taker, Eric Dier, shot the ball into the goal to take England through to the next round, Harry was overjoyed. This was a moment he'd dreamed of since he was a schoolboy!

Though his first World Cup campaign would end sooner than he hoped, rather than dwell on past mistakes, Harry was determined to use the experience as a learning curve. Spurs' star striker and England's hero still had a lot of goals left in his boots.

"When times are down, keep believing, keep working hard and things will pick up."

HARRY KANE

KANE'S
FIRST KICKS

Harry Edward Kane was born on 28 July 1993 at Whipps Cross Hospital, London, about five miles down the road from White Hart Lane, Tottenham Hotspur's home stadium. Harry's mum, Kim, was an assistant at a dental practice and his dad, Pat, owned a garage. Kim and Pat were loving and supportive, and Harry's big brother, Charlie, was his best friend growing up. The Kanes were a family of football fanatics and huge Spurs fans.

Almost as soon as he could walk, Harry was toddling down to the local park with Pat and Charlie for a kickabout. The small playing field wasn't exactly a world-class stadium. There were no nets or markings, and certainly no cheering crowds, but the trio made do with a patch of grass and a couple of trees for goalposts.

Harry quickly became as obsessed with football as the rest of his family, and a highlight of the week was going to see Spurs play at White Hart Lane. At his first match, four-year-old Harry sat in the crowd, proudly wearing his white-and-blue Spurs shirt, spellbound by the incredible players racing around the field below him. His favourite player, striker Teddy Sheringham, had just transferred to Manchester United. But as one of Tottenham's all-time highest goalscorers he was still Harry's hero, and his preferred footballer to copy at the park. After watching a match, Harry and Charlie practised the tricky tackles and skilful finishes they'd seen at the Lane.

A Sporting Start

When Harry was six the family moved to nearby Chingford, hometown of another legendary footballer, David Beckham. Harry dreamed of following in David's footsteps and becoming a sporting star himself, so when he spotted an advert for a trial at Ridgeway Rovers, the local club that David played for when he was a boy, Harry knew he had to go for it.

At the warm-up, the coach of Ridgeway Rovers, Dave Bricknell, introduced himself to the ten boys hoping to join his team and asked if anyone was up for having a go in goal. Harry preferred scoring goals to saving them, but he was keen to show the coach that he was happy to do anything, so he put his hand in the air to volunteer. Harry played well as a goalkeeper, making some skilful saves, and Dave was impressed. But then someone suggested that he should try Harry on the pitch – it turned out he was even better on the field than he was between the posts. Harry ran around the training ground, scoring goals from way down the field.

The trials were a success. Every week, Kim or Pat drove Harry to the nearby training ground, where he worked on improving his technique and building up his strength. He soon became Ridgeway Rovers' number-one striker.

Rubbing Shoulders with Rivals

Ridgeway Rovers had lots of strong players. Scouts from bigger clubs often came to watch their matches. Less than two years after Harry had joined the team, a scout invited him to a trial session for the youth academy of a Premier League club – it wasn't Harry's beloved Spurs, but their rivals, Arsenal! Still, the opportunity to play for such a strong team was too good to miss. Compared to Ridgeway Rovers' training ground, Arsenal's facilities were state-of-the art, with pristine pitches, gyms and meeting rooms.

Academy Trials

Big clubs like Arsenal and Tottenham Hotspur do not offer open trials. Instead, the clubs send out scouts, people whose job it is to search for talented players from local teams. Once a scout has spotted a player they think the club might be interested in, they make a recommendation, and the academy coaches might invite that player to a trial. At the trials, coaches look for players that can fill gaps in their current line-up, as well as someone with a strong technique and a personality that will fit in with the team.

Harry performed well at the trials and signed up with Arsenal for a whole season. He made the most of every opportunity, and though he wasn't as fast as some of the other boys, his powerful shots often found their mark. At the end of the season, however, there was bad news. On a walk to the park together, Pat put a hand on Harry's shoulder. "I've got to tell you something," he said. "Arsenal have released you." It meant that he wouldn't be continuing at the club. The coaches didn't think he was athletic enough and were worried about his pace.

Harry was disappointed. He'd done his best for the academy, even though his heart belonged to another club, and they had still decided to let him go. But Pat wasn't fazed, he told Harry that if they worked hard, he'd be chosen to play for another club soon enough.

Embarrassing Photo

Years later, when Harry was playing for Tottenham, Arsenal fans found an old photo of him wearing the Gunners' kit at the academy and shared it on the internet. They thought the photo proved Harry wasn't a true Spurs fan. But Harry hit back at his critics, saying, "I wanted to wear a Tottenham kit but I don't think that would've gone down too well. I was eight years old . . . I just wanted to play football."

SCHOOLBOY
SUPERSTAR

Harry returned to Ridgeway Rovers, who warmly welcomed back their star striker. Though his confidence had been knocked, rather than give up on becoming a world-class player, Harry was more determined than ever to achieve his dream. He wanted to prove that the Arsenal coaches were wrong. "It was probably the best thing that ever happened to me," he later said. "Because it gave me a drive that wasn't there before."

When he was eleven years old, Harry started at Chingford Foundation School, where David Beckham had also been a student, years before.

Every day Harry walked past David's Real Madrid shirt, framed above the reception desk.

Harry joined Chingford Foundation School's football team and was soon excelling in local tournaments. He was great at controlling the ball and getting it into the goal. His clever tactics meant that the opposing team's goalkeepers were always on edge when Harry was on the pitch! According to Mark Leadon, his PE teacher, "When he played for the school, he gave it everything. He was always technically gifted and a real team player."

Harry's goals soon led Chingford to school cup victory. And it wasn't just the football team that benefitted from Harry's sporting skills – he was also a very good cricketer and opened the bowling for the school's team.

Meeting a Hero

Though he was putting in lots of practice, there was further disappointment for Harry when he failed a trial for Tottenham Hotspur's youth academy. Because he was born in July, some of the other hopefuls in his age group were almost a year older, and Harry still had a lot of growing to do.

In the roads around their house, Harry, Charlie and their friends played football under the streetlights, using their bundled-up jumpers to mark goalposts. Sometimes, they'd hire a small local pitch for five-a-side matches. Once, the group was mid-game when a flashy black Range Rover pulled up. The door opened – and none other than Tottenham superstar Jermain Defoe stepped out! "Fancy a game?" the Spurs striker asked the gobsmacked boys.

Jermain got stuck in, keeping the ball away from the group with ease. Harry attempted a couple of cheeky tackles, but Jermain blocked him each time. Harry might have been an excellent player for his age, but he was no match against a Premiership legend!

Two More Trials

Towards the end of Year Seven, Harry was offered a trial at Watford. A scout for their youth academy had spotted the skilful schoolboy at a Ridgeway

Rovers game and saw some serious potential. Harry smashed the trial and was signed up as a youth team player. But it turned out that another club had their eyes on him – none other than Tottenham Hotspur.

Mark O'Toole, Spurs' youth scout, had been watching Harry for over a year. Though he saw that Harry was a gifted player, Mark wanted to make sure he was ready to join Spurs' academy. He'd failed his first trial there, after all. Harry wasn't big and he wasn't particularly fast – his technique would have to be perfect to earn him a spot on the Under-13s team.

Harry had only been with Watford for a few weeks when they took on Tottenham. Mark watched as the eleven-year-old player searched for opportunities to drive the ball home. He could see that Harry was completely focused and playing his heart out on the pitch. After the final whistle, Mark called Pat over for a chat. He wanted Harry to try out at Tottenham again. This time, Harry was determined it would be his last ever trial. He was going to get into Tottenham's academy, and he was going to stay there, no matter what it took.

Spurs, At Last

Harry made it through his trial with Tottenham and became a fully-fledged member of the Spurs youth team. But it wasn't going to be an easy ride. He might have been Ridgeway Rover's best striker, but the standard of football at Tottenham was much higher. Smaller, slower and weaker than some of the other boys, he struggled to shine during practice. Still, what he lacked in size and speed he made up for with bucketloads of enthusiasm. His early knocks had made him eager to prove himself. Harry listened to every piece of advice his coaches gave him and spent hours perfecting the techniques he hadn't yet mastered. The coaches came to see him as a reliable, enthusiastic young footballer with an excellent attitude, even if he wasn't yet their star player.

So, at the end of his first season, Harry was gutted to receive a letter telling him that he'd been released from his contract. He couldn't understand it, and nor could his family. Harry had been getting better and better, and his coaches seemed pleased with his improvement. Much to Harry's relief, Pat soon received a phone call from the academy. It seemed that Harry had been sent the wrong letter by mistake! Tottenham wanted him to stay on for another season, after all.

Later in 2005, Harry met another one of his football idols – David Beckham himself! David was launching his own football academy, and Harry was one of the lucky students from Chingford Foundation School selected to attend. Dressed in matching blue tracksuits, Harry and fifteen other boys and girls took part in a skills session under David's expert eye. It was a special moment, and another encouraging encounter that spurred Harry on to work harder.

STRIKING
FOR SPURS

"Just five more!" Harry said, lining up to take another shot at goal. It was the end of another practice session and his coach, Alex Inglethorpe, fished the ball out of the bushes from the young player's last attempt. Harry was always the first to arrive at practice and the last to leave. According to Alex, he was a dream student and "his own best coach". Harry often stayed behind for extra shooting practice with Alex after all the other boys had gone home.

Harry was making his way up through the age groups at Tottenham Hotspur's youth academy. Usually, Harry played in midfield, which meant he played in the central area of the pitch. He started off in a holding role, specializing in ball skills like passing, but was soon moved to a central attacking position.

But some of the training staff at Tottenham were still doubtful that Harry had what it took to make it. He had a great attitude, but they were concerned he wasn't big enough or fast enough to hold his own as he went up the age groups. Alex, Pat and Harry decided some extra training would help convince them, so Harry began working with a fitness instructor to improve his speed. Soon, the hard work paid off – his body began to change as his muscles strengthened and he transformed from a gangly schoolboy into a strong athlete.

As time went on and Harry became one of the youth team's key players, he couldn't take part in as many matches for his school, though he was always happy to step in if Chingford Foundation really needed him. When he wasn't training with Spurs, Harry went jogging around his neighbourhood to improve his fitness, or relaxed at home watching sports with Charlie, whether it was football, golf or cricket.

Travels with Tottenham

At fifteen years old, Harry was regularly starting for the Under-16s, but spent some time with the more senior Under-18s squad, playing alongside top talents including Andros Townsend and Ryan Mason. In January 2009, Harry was picked to play in the Copa Chivas tournament and swapped wintery Chingford for sunny Guadalajara, Mexico. He found the goal in his first two games, scoring against Norwegian side Stabæk Fotball and Mexican team CDSC Cruz Azul. Harry didn't play in the next two matches – Tottenham lost them both and were out of the tournament – but Harry stepped up to score again in the third-place play-off, making him the second-highest goalscorer in his team after Ryan. A few months later, he joined the team in Switzerland for Torneo Bellinzona. Though Harry didn't score, he helped his team to win the tournament by setting up some goals and enjoyed his time away with the club.

Sweet Sixteen

The summer of 2009 would turn out to be to one of the most important of Harry's life. He had finished Year 11 and passed his GCSEs so, now that school was over, he needed to make up his mind about what he wanted to do next. There was really only one option. He wanted to play football, and he wanted to play it professionally for Tottenham Hotspur.

The day he turned sixteen, no birthday present could rival the gift that Spurs gave him – a scholarship contract! Clearly his extra coaching and dedication had paid off.

Harry kicked off the 2009–10 season with four goals in his first four games at the Eurofoot tournament. His opening matches in the Premier Academy League weren't so successful, and Harry went four matches without finding the goal. But on his fifth match against Fulham, Harry netted. He went on to score against Bristol in the next game, and not one but two of his shots found their mark in a game against Watford the following month.

Spurs' first-team coach, Harry Redknapp, had been keeping an eye on the young striker and picked him as a substitute for a match against Everton. It was Harry's first time on the bench, and though he didn't get to play, he was inspired by the experience of training alongside the first-team professionals. By December, Harry had nine Premier League Academy goals under his belt,, and was the top scorer for the Under-18s. His efforts earned him the position of team captain.

Country Call-up

At the start of 2010, Harry got some more good news. His strong performances had caught the eye of John Peacock, the England Under-17s coach. John invited Harry to join the England squad for the Algarve Tournament in Portugal. Though Harry didn't score in the two matches he played – against France and Ukraine – he was proud to wear the Three Lions on his shirt for the first time and be part of the winning team. The Under-17s European Championships were just around the corner, and Harry hoped his stellar performances with Spurs would earn him a place on the squad again. Sadly, it wasn't to be. Though he helped the team to qualify, Harry missed out on the finals due to illness and was forced to watch the team's ultimate victory while recovering at home.

Once he was feeling better, Harry returned to training. That summer, he signed his first professional contract with Spurs and began regularly training with the senior first team, which included incredible world-class players like Gareth Bale, Roman Pavlyuchenko, Peter Crouch, and his childhood hero Jermain Defoe! Jermain even remembered Harry from their spontaneous street kickabout.

Harry was repeatedly proving that he could be a reliable striker, with a good understanding of the game as a whole and an ability to spot opportunities other players might miss. He'd scored eighteen goals in twenty-two games for Tottenham's Under-18s, but with top-class strikers Jermain, Roman and Peter already on the first team, there was just no room for Harry in the senior squad. How was he ever going to make his mark at the club if he couldn't even get on to the pitch?

OUT ON LOAN

Harry may have just signed a new contract, but he needed practice in senior games, and he wasn't going to get it at Tottenham. The Spurs coaches decided to send him out on loan to another club for a spell in the lower leagues. There, he'd get lots of pitch time, and a chance to prove himself as a footballer worth his grit, away from the glitz and glamour of the Premier League. Harry must have been disappointed that his club were sending him away, but it wasn't unusual for players to spend time with other teams. With his usual determination, Harry was keen to make the most of the opportunity.

English Football League System

England's football system is split up into tiers of interconnected leagues. The top three tiers are:

The Premier League
Teams: Twenty
Relegation: The bottom three teams are relegated to the Championship League at the end of the season

English Football League Championship
Teams: Twenty-four
Promotion: At the end of the season the top two teams are automatically promoted to the Premier League, the next four compete in play-offs with the winner gaining the third promotion spot
Relegation: The bottom three teams are relegated to League One

English Football League One

Teams: Twenty-four

Promotion: The top two teams are automatically promoted to the Championship League, the next four compete in play-offs with the winner gaining the third promotion spot

Relegation: The bottom four teams are relegated to League Two

Off to the Orient

In early 2011, Harry arrived at Leyton Orient, then a League One team, where he would spend the rest of the season. His debut (first) match, a game against Rochdale at Spotland, was held on a grey January day where heavy rain had turned the pitch into a mud-pit. "Welcome to League One!" Leyton Orient's captain, Scott McGleish, told Harry when he saw the Tottenham player staring worriedly at the boggy grass. He definitely wasn't at White Hart Lane any more!

Despite the awful weather, seventeen-year-old Harry made a seventeen-minute appearance, crashing on to the pitch as a substitute for Scott towards the end of the second half. If Leyton Orient fans thought that this big club player might consider himself above their team, they needn't have worried; Harry proved instantly that he was willing to get down and very dirty on the boggy pitch. "I was determined to show what I could do and here was my chance," Harry said a few years later.

In his first home game, Harry scored from inside the six-yard box, hitting the ball into the top-right corner of the goal and helping his temporary team to a 4–0 finish against Sheffield Wednesday. Harry was smaller than many of the players he was up against, some of whom had a decade's more experience than him, but he was not afraid to throw himself into the thick of it, even going in for a dangerous header in a match against Huddersfield where there was a chance he could have been seriously hurt! In total, Harry made eighteen appearances for Leyton Orient, scoring five goals. At the end of the season, Harry went back to Spurs, a little older, a little stronger, and ready to prove himself in their senior team.

Childhood Sweetheart

Before he returned to White Hart Lane, Harry went on holiday with his new girlfriend, Kate Goodland. The pair had been friends since primary school and had both attended Chingford Foundation – in fact, Kate was among the group of students selected to meet David Beckham at his football academy launch back in 2005. A photo of Harry and Kate standing either side of David even made the newspaper. They'd started dating during Harry's time at Leyton Orient. Despite Harry's busy schedule, they spent as much time together as they could, and soon fell in love.

Like Harry, Kate was sports mad. She would go on to study sports science at university, before becoming a fitness instructor. Kate's brother was a huge fan of American football and introduced Harry to the sport. The National Football League (NFL) would come to play a big part in Harry's life.

Making Moves at Millwall

The 2011 UEFA Europa League provided a good opportunity for Harry Redknapp to give his younger players some game time, as the first team was tied up in the Premier League. In his opening match against Hearts, Harry was gutted to miss a penalty, the goalkeeper confidently blocking his shot, but he redeemed himself later in the tournament with a last-minute goal against Shamrock Rovers – his first professional goal for Spurs.

Still, when January 2012 came around, Harry was sent away on loan again. This time he went to Millwall, along with fellow Spurs teammate, Ryan Mason. There was much at stake for Millwall – the South London team were struggling and faced getting relegated from the Championship. They desperately needed talented strikers like Harry.

The season began for Harry with a 1–0 loss at Bristol City, followed by a painful 6–0 loss against Birmingham at home. But by February, Harry was on form and began racking up the goals. He scored against Burnley and again at Peterborough. Soon, Millwall's relegation fears were behind them, thanks in part to Harry's excellent efforts. Well liked by both the team and the fans – who had been known to sometimes throw things on the pitch if they didn't agree with the ref's decision! – Harry enjoyed his time with Millwall, valuing the opportunity to play in tough games that really mattered.

Harry was named Millwall's Young Player of the Season. He'd scored an important seven goals in twenty-two Championship appearances. Kenny Jackett, Millwall's manager, praised Harry's efforts, saying, "I felt he came here as a boy and is a man now."

A TOUGH YEAR

Over the summer of 2012, Harry joined the England Under-19s for the European Championships in Estonia, where he scored against France to help England to a 2–1 victory. There would be no more glory in the competition, however, as England lost the semi-final against Greece and Harry, stuck on the bench, could do nothing to help.

No Luck at Norwich

When Harry returned to White Hart Lane at the start of the season, Harry Redknapp had been replaced by former Chelsea manager, André Villas-Boas. After impressing his new boss with three goals, known as a hat-trick, in a friendly game against Southend, Harry got his first brief taste of Premiership football, coming on in the eighty-fifth minute of Spurs' opening match against Newcastle. Tottenham were 2–1 down, and as soon as Harry was out on the field he was looking to get the equaliser, but it wasn't to be – hardly surprising as he had less than ten minutes of play! Still, he'd been on the pitch in a Premiership game. It was another first to tick off his list on the way to becoming Tottenham's star.

But his season with Spurs was over before it had really begun. Just a few weeks later, Harry found himself on loan again – this time to Norwich City. It seemed there *still* wasn't room for him in Tottenham's senior squad. After just two appearances, however, Harry was forced to return to White Hart Lane early. He'd fallen awkwardly on his ankle during the second half of a game against Doncaster and had to be carried off on a stretcher. It turned out to be a nasty fracture to his metatarsal, a bone in his foot, and it looked like Harry would need a couple of months to recover. Over the following weeks,

Harry tried to be patient and listen to the doctors' advice. Though the recovery exercises were boring, Harry knew they were the quickest way back on to the pitch. By December, he was ready to rejoin Norwich, but sadly didn't find the net in his next three games, though he wasn't given much time on the pitch to do so.

Lonely in Leicester

Seeing that the loan wasn't working out for their budding striker, André Villas-Boas called Harry back to White Hart Lane – only to send him out again three weeks later! Harry's next loan spell was at Leicester City, and it started promisingly with a goal in Leicester's 3–0 win against Blackburn. But a two-month dry spell followed, where Harry hardly got any play time at all. Often sitting beside him on the substitute bench was another player struggling to get time on the pitch – Jamie Vardy. The two young men couldn't know that, in just a few years' time, they would be starring for England together!

The constant back-and-forth was taking its toll, and Harry began to feel really down. Alone in his flat in Leicester, miles from friends and family, he had a horrible thought. *If I can't even play for Leicester in the Championship,* Harry worried, *how am I supposed to play for Spurs in the Premiership?* He felt so low that when his family came over to visit, Harry told them he wanted to give up. But Pat wouldn't hear of it. He gave Harry the same advice he had when Arsenal had dropped him, all those years ago. "Keep working – keep doing," Pat told his son. "And everything will be all right."

A few weeks later, Harry came across an inspirational documentary that gave him further encouragement. As a fan of American football, Harry often watched YouTube clips of his favourite team, the New England Patriots. He stumbled upon a programme about the quarterback Tom Brady, one of the NFL's top players. Harry was surprised to discover that – like him – Tom had been overlooked time and time again early on his career. Despite the bumps in the road, the quarterback's self-belief saw him come out on top. Harry was reminded of himself. Like Tom, he'd had to fight for his place, working relentlessly to prove he was good enough. Harry promised himself that he would continue to train harder than anyone else until he got his big chance.

The season ended in tears for Leicester as they failed to earn a promotion. Harry hadn't been able to help them reach the Premier League. Then again, they hadn't really given him the chance.

World Cup Woes

Before the 2013–14 season started, Harry joined the England Under-20s squad as they prepared for the Under-20s World Cup in Turkey. It was fun getting to know the other players, and Harry made the whole squad laugh when he turned up for a team-building trip dressed in full golfing gear! There were few opportunities for celebration during the tournament though. Harry had several personal highs, including setting up a goal against Iraq with a skilled header, and scoring against Chile with a neat shot to the bottom corner from outside the penalty area. But overall, the team performed poorly and were knocked out at the group stage. At the end of their campaign, Harry was glad to be heading back to the Lane. He just hoped that, this time, it would be for good.

FIGHTING FOR A START

Back at White Hart Lane, with Gareth Bale sold, André Villas-Boas decided that the team needed another striker. Rather than looking to the young men coming up through the academy ranks, he paid a record twenty-six million pounds for high-scoring Spaniard Roberto Soldado. This was bad news for Harry. It was unlikely André would take a risk with an inexperienced player like himself in Premiership games, rather than the top professional he'd just forked out millions for.

In fact, André was soon considering sending Harry out on loan yet again! The manager told the young striker that there were several Premiership clubs interested in him. But Harry didn't want to just play in the Premier League. He wanted to play in the Premier League *for Spurs*. Harry decided to stand his ground and told André that he didn't want to go. He wanted to stay at the Lane and prove to his boss that he had what it took to be in the starting line-up, week in, week out.

Changes at the Lane

Though André agreed to let the plucky striker stay, Harry's dream of regularly starting for Spurs didn't happen overnight. He made it on to the pitch just six times before the end of the year, scoring once in a League Cup game after Jermain Defoe passed him the ball. It was hardly the dramatic entrance to the world of Premiership football he was hoping for. In December 2013, after a disappointing performance in the first half of the season, Tottenham fired André as manager. A 5–0 defeat by Liverpool at Spurs' home ground had been the last straw.

Tim Sherwood, a former youth coach, was the new man in charge, signing a contract until the end of the season. Tim knew Harry well, and had worked closely with him in the Under-21s, but that didn't mean he was willing to risk his new position, and reputation, by putting the young striker on the pitch before he was ready. Tim was fresh to senior management, so it is perhaps unsurprising that he was cautious, sticking with expensive Roberto and tried-and-tested Emmanuel Adebayor, who had been playing for Tottenham since 2011.

Not long after Tim took over as manager, Jermain signed with Toronto FC and said goodbye to White Hart Lane in January 2014. Jermain's parting gift to Harry was his number 18 shirt. "You're a natural goalscorer," Jermain told him.

The Premier League Competition Format

The football season runs from August to May. Throughout the season, each club plays every other Premier League club twice – once at their opponents' stadium and once at their home stadium – for a total of thirty-eight games. The team's ranking is based on their total points, then goal difference and then goals scored. The points are awarded as follows:

Win: three points
Draw: one point
Loss: no points

A First Start

It wasn't until 7 April 2014 that Tim Sherwood gave Harry his opportunity. After four months on the bench, his chance to start in a Premiership game finally came. The match against Sunderland was being held on a rainy day on Tottenham's home turf. Harry was thrilled to be on the pitch as the starting whistle blew, but the crowd were not so pleased to see him. At half-time, with the score at 1–1, some of them even began chanting for Roberto Soldado (who had been left out of the starting line-up) to come on.

But at fifty-nine minutes, Christian Eriksen curled a cross into the six-yard box ... and Harry tapped it into the bottom corner of the goal! The crowd went wild – they weren't singing for Roberto any more. Harry had scored for Spurs in his first ever Premiership start. He was overcome with emotion – relief, pride, and so much joy!

WHAM! Harry came back down to Earth with a bump! He'd crashed heads with a Sunderland player as the pair crossed paths at full speed. The medical teams quickly patched them up and Harry returned to the pitch with a bandage wrapped around his head. The match finished 5–1 to Tottenham. Tim was delighted with the team's performance, showering Harry with praise in his post-match press interview. "He got his opportunity and he took it with both hands," Tim said, before adding with a smile: "Get ready for Saturday, Harry, 'cause you're playing." For Harry it was the best moment of his career so far.

True to his word, Tim started Harry in the next Premiership match against West Bromwich, where Harry scored once again. A week later, he made it three games in a row, with an expert header. Harry didn't manage to score in the next three matches, but he was off to an excellent start. Tottenham ended the season sixth in the Premier League.

Over the summer, England crashed out of the World Cup disappointingly early, finishing bottom of the group with a dreary goalless draw against Costa Rica. Harry dreamed that one day he would be out there on a World Cup pitch, helping his team to a happier ending.

A BREAKTHROUGH
SEASON

By the start of the next season (2014–15), Tottenham had another new manager. Tim Sherwood was out, and Argentinian Mauricio Pochettino was in. Mauricio was keen to improve a Spurs team struggling in the league tables. For a few months, it looked like Harry was going to be back on the bench for Premier League games, as Mauricio gave Roberto and Emmanuel another chance to prove themselves. Harry was, however, playing in lots of League Cup and Europa League games, and regularly coming on as substitute during Premiership matches.

Harry claimed the first professional hat-trick of his career in a Europa League game against Greek side Asteras Tripolis, with two shots and a header. Despite the heroics, he ended the night red-cheeked. Just a few minutes before the final whistle, Spurs' goalkeeper was sent off with a red card, so Harry took his place between the posts . . . only to immediately let in the only Greek goal of the game from a tame free kick! "It was a great night until I went in goal," Harry joked to reporters after the match. "I think I'll leave that to the keepers from now on!"

On 2 November 2014, Harry came on as a substitute in a Spurs match against Aston Villa, scoring with a spectacular free kick that flicked in off the head of a Villa defender; this brought his scoring run to seven goals in seven games. Talking to the press after the Aston Villa match, Mauricio admitted, "He maybe deserves to play in the Premier League more." Spurs fans took to social media to demand that Mauricio give Harry his first Premier League start of the season.

Brady and Wilson

In October 2014, Kate and Harry welcomed two Labrador puppies, one yellow and one black, into their home. Harry named the yellow pup Brady after his NFL idol, Tom Brady, and Kate named the black pup Wilson – which also happens to be the surname of a legendary NFL player, Russell Wilson! They quickly became a huge part of Harry's life.

Earning His Spurs

It wasn't until 9 November that Harry got his first Premier League start of the 2014–15 season. The game didn't go well for Tottenham, ending in a 2–1 defeat, but Mauricio stuck with Harry in the starting line-up for the next match. This time, Harry scored, helping Tottenham to a 2–1 win against Hull City. From that point forward, Mauricio decided that Harry would start every Premiership game he was fit for. He'd finally made it.

By December, Tottenham Hotspur seemed to have turned a corner, winning or drawing in five out of their six league fixtures. As the New Year dawned, Harry's substitute bench woes were a long way behind him, and he was ready to take his place as a Tottenham legend. In a headline-making match against top-of-the-league Chelsea, Harry helped Spurs to a 5–3 victory by scoring two goals, proving that one of the strongest defences in the world was no match for his fancy footwork. Harry was named Premier League Player of the Month in recognition of his impressive performance in January.

Perhaps the most significant game of the season for Harry came on 7 February. The match was against Arsenal, the team that had released him at eight years old for not being athletic enough. *It's taken me twelve years, but we'll see who was right and who was wrong,* Harry thought to himself in the tunnel before the match. Soon Harry came close to scoring with a well-aimed long-range shot, but the goalkeeper got safe hands on the ball. Early in the second half, Harry hovered near the far post while teammate Mousa Dembélé took a corner. As the ball was flicked towards him, Harry took his chance and tapped it into the goal. It was an incredible moment, and the joy was clear on Harry's face as he raced towards the stands to celebrate. But the superstar striker wasn't finished yet. With just four minutes left of the game, Harry produced what he called "probably the best header I've ever scored", slamming the ball into the back of the net and taking Tottenham to a 2–1 victory. Harry dived to the ground in celebration and was soon lost among the limbs of his teammates, all desperate to embrace the man who had helped to beat their biggest rivals. The sound from the stands was deafening, and as Harry did a lap of the stadium, the fans began to sing their new favourite chant:

"He's one of our own,
He's one of our own,
Harry Kane,
He's one of our own!"

At the end of February, Harry was named Premier League Player of the month once again.

Scoring for England

Present at the Arsenal versus Tottenham match was none other than Roy Hodgson, the manager of the England seniors' team. Harry had previously played well for the country's youth squads, and his recent performances proved that he deserved a shot on the first team. In March 2015, Harry made his debut for the seniors against Lithuania under the bright lights of Wembley Stadium. He joined the action as a second-half substitute and was on the pitch for just seventy-nine seconds before he scored. Raheem Sterling crossed from the left and Harry, always in the right place at the right time, headed the ball into the goal. Harry wasn't one to play it cool when he scored, throwing his arms wide and yelling with triumph, as if he was a supporter.

"When people saw me celebrating a goal, that pure emotion and happiness and joy, I think that's what people enjoyed," he later reflected. "Like a fan on the pitch." The captain of the England team, Wayne Rooney, told the press that Harry's presence was "a great lift for the nation". For Harry, it was a dream come true.

End of the Season

On 21 March 2015, Harry delivered three goals in a match against his former loan team, Leicester. That made him the first Spurs player to score a hat-trick in the Premier League since Gareth Bale. Unfortunately, by the end of the month, Tottenham were out of the Europa League and FA Cup, so only had the Premiership to focus on. It just wasn't their season – Spurs finished fifth in the Premier League, a disappointing result considering their run of spectacular matches at the beginning of the year, but Harry ended the season with a winning goal against Everton, sending a strong message to fans and rivals. To top it off, Harry won the Professional Footballers' Association (PFA) Young Player of the Year Award.

GOALS,
GOALS, GOALS

At the start of the 2015–16 season, Mauricio made some big changes to the team. He sold Roberto Soldado and released Emmanuel Adebayor. Harry was now not only Spurs' number-one striker, but pretty much their only striker! He swapped his shirt number from 18 to 10 – though Jermain's number had meant a lot to him, now that 10 was available, he couldn't resist the chance to take the number worn by so many of his idols, including Robbie Keane and Teddy Sheringham.

It was a tough start to the football year for Harry, and he went a month without scoring. During the summer, Harry had also suffered a disappointing Euros tournament with the Under-21s. The press began to speculate that he was simply a "one-season wonder". But Harry kept his cool, channelling the self-confidence that had been so important throughout his career.

After curling the ball into the top corner in a game against Manchester City, Harry's goal drought seemed to be over. But a month later, Harry accidentally scored in the *wrong* net, heading in an own goal against Swansea. The Welsh fans turned Tottenham's favourite chant on them, declaring that Harry Kane was one of *their* own. Mauricio was disappointed that Spurs had tied the game (2–2), but he told the press, "Harry does not need to worry about it. He does a lot for the team."

A Slick Side

Though he'd sold two forwards, Mauricio had also taken on some new players at the start of the season, including attacking midfielder Dele Alli and winger Son Heung-min. The fresh players brought great energy, and by the end of October, Spurs had found their stride with Harry delivering another stunning hat-trick this time in a game against Bournemouth.

Harry got the ball in the net in the next three Spurs games, including scoring against rivals Arsenal, though disappointingly he couldn't win the match for his team this time and had to settle for a 1–1 draw. It quickly became clear that the striker was no one-season wonder, but a sharp professional with a clever understanding of the game and a killer technique. In December, he made his one hundredth appearance for Spurs, marking the moment with a goal against Southampton, and on Boxing Day, he broke Teddy Sheringham's record of twenty-six goals in a calendar year. "He's an outstanding player," Harry's hero, Sheringham, remarked to the press. "He can do everything I could do but he's got a bit of pace as well. He can go a long way."

Highs and Lows

In March 2016, even a broken nose gained in a game against Crystal Palace wasn't going to stop Harry playing for England as they faced off against Germany. The match may have been a friendly, but Harry didn't hold back – he took control of the ball as it dropped nearby from a corner, dodged two opponents and performed a skilled forward feint before quickly turning and driving a shot into the far corner. It was the most spectacular goal of his career so far.

After such a promising start to the season, Tottenham's campaign took a turn for the worse. At the beginning of May, just three games stood between them and the top of the Premier League – they would need to win all three to be crowned champions. But in their first match against Chelsea, Tottenham only managed to scrape a 2–2 draw. A few players seemed to lose their heads, and the Spurs team were handed nine yellow cards – the most for a single team in a match in Premier League history. They then faced a 2–1 loss to Southampton and took a 5–1 thrashing from Newcastle. Not only did they miss out on the Premier League title but they even finished below Arsenal.

But it wasn't all doom and gloom. As the 2015–16 season came to a close, Harry Kane, with twenty-five Premiership goals, was awarded the Premier League Golden Boot. The "one-season wonder" had come back to score the most goals in the entire tournament – and he was ready to do it again next year.

Heartbreak at the Euros

Harry's stunning season with Spurs earned him a place on the England team for the European Championships over the summer of 2016 in France. It was his first major international tournament. He was on a team with world-class players including Wayne Rooney, Jamie Vardy and Raheem Sterling, along with Spurs teammates Dele Alli and Eric Dier. The England manager Roy Hodgson had booked an entire five-star hotel for the England team – each player had an Xbox or PlayStation set up in their room, and there was a fancy golf course under a mile away. England had qualified with ten wins out of ten, and the country had high expectations.

The first group stage game was against Russia. Harry failed to get the ball anywhere near the goal and the match ended 1–1. In one of the most controversial decisions of the tournament, Roy had selected Harry to take corners, removing the team's best forward from the penalty box at some of the most crucial moments.

The next match was against Wales on 16 June. Harry was in the starting line-up, but after missing a few chances early on in the game, he was pulled from the pitch. The team went on to win 2–1, but it was hardly a comfortable victory. The last goal came just three minutes before the final whistle. The press wondered whether, after such an incredible season for Spurs, Harry was exhausted and unable to play to his usual standard. After all, as Tottenham's sole striker, there had been a lot of his weight on his shoulders during last season's campaign. Harry was kept on the bench for the final match against Slovakia and the team finished with a disappointing 0–0 draw.

But the England versus Iceland match turned out to be the biggest humiliation of the tournament. Iceland, thirty-fourth in the world, managed to defeat England 2–1. Former footballer Alan Shearer thought the performance was one of England's worst ever. "We were outthought, we were outfought, we were outbattled and we were totally hopeless," he told BBC's *Match of the Day*. Harry and the team were out of the Euros and Roy Hodgson resigned as England manager.

Even going on holiday with Dele, Eric and their partners couldn't take Harry's mind off things, and he struggled to get over the disappointing and painful end to the tournament. But Harry would make sure to learn from his mistakes and move forward. Spurs' next season was starting soon, after all.

EXCITING TIMES
AT THE LANE

Harry had a lot to aim for in the 2016–17 season. Having come third in the Premiership in 2015–16, Tottenham had qualified for the Champions League. A new season also meant another stab at the Premier League, and Harry was likely to be called up for the World Cup qualifying matches.

The Champions League

The Union of European Football Associations (UEFA) Champions League is an annual competition for top-division clubs across Europe. Thirty-two clubs compete in the main group stage, split into groups of four clubs who play each of their opponents twice (home and away). The top two teams in each group (sixteen in total) advance to the knockout stages. For the round of sixteen, the quarter-finals and the semi-finals, each team plays at home and away. The finals are held a neutral venue and the triumphant team wins the iconic European Champion Clubs' Cup.

Mauricio bought a new player, Vincent Janssen, so Harry would no longer be the team's sole striker. The partnership seemed to work well from the off, with both Harry and Vincent scoring in a pre-season game against Inter Milan. But a month's goal drought followed, just as it had at the start of the previous season. Harry was not worried. He knew the goals would come even if it took a few weeks. "I didn't score in my first seven or eight games last season and then to go on and win the Golden Boot proves that it was just a matter of time," he told the press, before demonstrating his point by scoring in the very next game against Stoke.

The following week, Harry scored his second goal of the season against Sunderland, but limped off the pitch a few minutes before the final whistle, and was later carried away on a stretcher. He'd twisted his ankle after going in for an aggressive tackle. He needed to stay off the pitch for eight weeks while he recovered. He ended up missing ten Tottenham games, and though Vincent tried to fill Harry's shoes, the Spurs team struggled without their star striker.

Harry returned to play in the North London Derby against Arsenal on 6 November – a match he wasn't going to miss if he could help it! Though he didn't last the whole game, Harry shot a penalty into the centre of the net, and the match ended 1–1. Tottenham were knocked out of the Champions League not long after – their dreams of conquering Europe would have to wait. For now, they had the Premier League to focus on.

Harry's Healthy Lifestyle

Since December 2016, Harry has had his own personal chef. The top-class cook helps him to consume nutritionally balanced food and works around Harry's training schedule.

Harry's typical menu:

Breakfast
Omelette with brown toast and a side of spinach

Lunch
Chicken breast with asparagus

Dinner
Fish with broccoli and sweet potato

Snacks
Nuts, seeds and fresh fruit

Harry rarely eats unhealthy food, but does enjoy a plate of chips or a chocolate bar on very special occasions! He never drinks alcohol during the football season. Even though he has a personal chef, Harry enjoys cooking when he has the time, and his signature dish is chicken paella.

Starting a Family

On 8 January 2017, Harry and Kate welcomed their daughter Ivy Jane Kane to the world. Harry took to fatherhood straightaway. The sleepless nights weren't as bad as he thought they would be, and changing nappies was no problem! The pressures of parenthood certainly weren't affecting his football. On 26 February, Kate posted a photo of their new daughter with the caption, "My daddy has scored three hat-tricks since I've been born." Perhaps little Ivy was Harry's lucky charm!

Farewell to the Lane

With his ankle better, Harry was back on form. Even an injury scare in March – another knock to that same ankle – couldn't keep him off the pitch for long. By mid-April, he was once again in the running for the Golden Boot. A 2–0 win against Arsenal on 30 April ensured that Tottenham would finish ahead of their rivals for the first time since 1995. Towards the end of the season, Harry's scoring seemed to slow down, and Tottenham's dreams of topping the Premiership were dashed as they lost 1–0 to West Ham, putting them seven points behind Chelsea. But in his final few games, Harry made sure fans were in no doubt that he hadn't lost his touch, with four goals against Leicester and a hat-trick against Hull.

As the season drew to a close, the Spurs team prepared to leave White Hart Lane. Their home ground was being demolished in order to build a bigger and better stadium. While the work got underway, Spurs' temporary home would be Wembley, the largest football stadium in the country.

On 14 May, Tottenham played their final match at the Lane against Manchester United. "It's great to have been a part of the history here and I've had some special moments at this stadium," Harry commented before kick-off. "Today's game will be the end of an era." Early in the second half, Harry added one more "special moment" to his list: he became the last Spurs player ever to score at the old stadium. After the final whistle, forty-eight former club legends came on to the pitch, including Harry's childhood heroes, Teddy Sheringham and Robbie Keane. The crowd went wild.

Though Wembley was an exciting place to play, with a world-class pitch, it was strange for the Tottenham team to leave behind their beloved White Hart Lane. Still, when over 70,000 fans turned up to watch their first match, the atmosphere was incredible. The crowd erupted in deafening cheers and the wall of sound didn't diminish, even when the game against Chelsea finished with a 2–1 defeat, ending a nineteen-game home Premier League unbeaten run.

Harry secured the Golden Boot for the second year running. Not bad, considering his slow start to the season and the weeks of injuries! Harry's final tally was twenty-nine Premier League goals, and a total of thirty-five goals in thirty-eight appearances. Though there were rumours that Harry would transfer to one of the big European clubs, he signed a contract to stay with Spurs until 2020. His heart belonged to Tottenham, and it always would.

A RECORD-
BREAKING YEAR

As with the previous two seasons, Harry's 2017–18 campaign began with a dry spell, and he was unable to get a goal in August. But, just like in previous years, he soon found his stride. On 1 September, after scoring twice in England's 4–0 win against Malta, Harry jokingly tweeted that he "didn't like August anyway!" His streak continued with two goals against Everton in a Premier League match and two against Borussia Dortmund in Tottenham's Champions League opener. At the end of September, he was once again named Premier League Player of the Month.

But at the start of October, Harry faced a tough test when he captained the England team during their World Cup qualifier again Slovenia. "Come on!" Harry muttered to himself as he struggled to find a way to break through and take the ball towards the goal. Harry and his teammates were finding it difficult to get past Slovenia's defences and the crowd was starting to get restless. By the second half, some of the fans had become so bored they were entertaining themselves by throwing paper aeroplanes around the stands! Luckily, four minutes into injury time, Harry finally got his chance. He shot the ball into goal to take England to a 1–0 finish. The players were relieved to qualify for the World Cup, as was England's new manager, Gareth Southgate. Still, other than Harry's goal, the match had been a little dull. With the disappointment of the Euros still fresh in everyone's minds, hopes weren't particularly high for the summer.

However, even after two further injuries, 2017 proved to be a record-breaking year for the twenty-four-year-old striker. Harry became the first Premier League player to score seven hat-tricks in a calendar year, and his thirty-nine league goals for Spurs saw him surpass Alan Shearer's total of thirty-six for Blackburn Rovers in 1995. Harry was Europe's top goalscorer for 2017, and the press began to liken him to football legends Lionel Messi and Cristiano Ronaldo, but Harry didn't want get ahead of himself. "When you look at Messi and Ronaldo, I've obviously still got a long way before I can be compared to them," he said. "I want to keep improving and be up there one day."

Harry started the New Year with a four-game scoring run, bagging two goals against AFC Wimbledon and Everton, and goals against Southampton and Newport County. In February, he scored his one hundredth Premier League goal from the penalty spot in a match against Liverpool. Tottenham crashed out of the Champions League in March, and Harry suffered another injury that same month. Luckily, the damage wasn't too bad and he returned to first-team training after a few weeks of rest and recovery.

Kane's Kicks

To commemorate Harry's one hundredth Premier League goal, Nike produced a pair of personalized football boots. Designed in Spurs' blue and white, with flashes of gold, the boots have "100" written on each heel, and the insole bears the message "Keep it Kane".

By the end of the season, Harry had scored thirty goals in thirty-seven appearances. He'd beaten his previous season's record but was pipped to the post for the Golden Boot by Liverpool's Mohamed Salah, who finished with an incredible tally of thirty-two goals. Sadly, there were still no cups for Tottenham, who now hadn't lifted one for ten years, but they finished the Premier League in third place and once again qualified for the Champions League.

Captain Kane

At the start of May, Gareth Southgate told Harry he was making him captain for England's World Cup campaign. Harry was filled with pride – it was a moment he'd dreamed about since he was a kid playing football in the park. Harry had to keep the news a secret for several weeks and was only allowed to share it with his immediate family. Pat, Kim, Charlie and Kate were incredibly excited – they had no doubt that Harry was going to take the team to great heights! On 22 May 2018, the news became public. Gareth told the press, "Harry has some outstanding personal qualities. One of the most important things for a captain is that they set the standard every day."

World Cup Wonder

The England team flew out to St Petersburg, Russia, on 12 June 2018. They were staying in Repino, a quiet village nestled in the middle of a pine forest about nineteen miles outside of St Petersburg. The England manager hoped that a peaceful base would help his team relax in between tough games. Kate and Harry were expecting their second baby in a couple of months' time, so Kate was unable to join him, but Pat, Kim and Charlie flew out to be near the action. Harry was glad to have his family close by for the most important tournament of his career.

England and the FIFA World Cup

The FIFA World Cup is the biggest international football competition in the world. It is split into two parts, with the qualification phase taking place over three years and the finals occurring every fourth year. England have competed at the FIFA World Cup since 1950. Out of eighteen tournaments, England have failed to qualify for the finals three times and been knocked out at the group stages three times. England came fourth in 1990 and 2018, and have won the World Cup trophy once, in 1966.

FOR KANE AND COUNTRY

More than 13.7 million viewers around the United Kingdom watched England's first match of the World Cup finals against Tunisia on 18 June 2018. After just eleven minutes of play, England's John Stones nearly snatched a first goal with a nifty header. Tunisia's goalkeeper made an impressive save, but Harry reacted swiftly to the rebound, slotting the ball home! The delighted England team piled on top of their captain – thanks to Harry, they'd got their first goal in the World Cup finals! But the game took a turn for the worse when Tunisia equalized with a penalty. One minute into injury time, with a powerful whip of his head, Harry Kane knocked the ball into the net again, becoming the first England player to score two goals in a World Cup match since Gary Lineker in 1990. As the team celebrated on the pitch, the cameras flicked to an overjoyed Gareth Southgate leaping up and punching the air.

Kate cheered on her partner from their home in Essex. She had set up a tepee in the garden, decorated with England flags and fairy lights, packed full of comfy bean bags, and with a huge TV screen for her and Harry's friends to watch the matches on. Ivy wore a personalized England shirt, with the word *DADDY* on the back.

Rest and Recovery

After the game, the victorious England team flew back to their hotel in Repino and focused on getting mentally and physically ready for their next match. Harry splashed into an ice bath to help his muscles recover and relaxed by playing a few rounds of table tennis with his teammates. Some of the other England players were obsessed with Fortnite, and spent their free time glued to the screens in their room.

The next match against Panama turned out to be easy in comparison to their last game, with the Central American team nowhere near the same standard as the slick English side. Harry became the third England player to score a hat-trick at a World Cup, his three goals helping the team to a 6–1 finish. Harry was rested for the final match in the group stages, which England lost 0–1 to Belgium. They had finished second in their group and would go on to play Colombia in the round of sixteen.

Down to Penalties

Over the next few days, Gareth and Harry put their heads together to come up with a strategy to beat the Colombians in their next match. But what England's manager and captain hadn't accounted for was the opposing team's dirty tactics! From headbutting midfielder Jordan Henderson to arguing with the referee and delaying play, the Colombian team tried every nasty trick in the book to beat the England squad, and Harry alone was fouled nine times! Even the managers were at it, with one of Colombia's coaches deliberately knocking into

Raheem Sterling's shoulder as he walked off the pitch at half-time. Professional Raheem just gave him a hard stare, but the atmosphere was spiky.

At fifty-four minutes, after a Colombian player wrapped his arms around Harry, pulling him to the ground, the referee awarded England a penalty. Calm and collected, Harry stepped up to take the shot. One of the Colombian players had sneakily scuffed up the penalty spot, but it made no difference to Harry as he rocketed the ball into the net, scoring his sixth goal of the tournament.

After a Colombian equalizer, the match went to extra time. Neither team managed to score again so they moved on to a penalty shootout. England had never had much luck with those in the past.

Harry was the first England player to step up to the mark, after Colombia's first successful shot. He took a steadying breath, ran through his usual routine and confidently directed the ball into the bottom corner of the net. The following two England players followed suit with goals, as did the next two Colombians, but it looked like the curse of the penalty shootout was set to continue as Jordan Henderson's shot was saved, giving the Colombians a 3–2 lead.

All was not lost. The next Colombian player's shot hit the bar, putting England back in the running, and Kieran Trippier took the score to 3–3. But it was the England goalkeeper, Jordan Pickford, who salvaged the shootout, making a crucial save against Colombia's last penalty taker. Eric Dier put the South American team's World Cup dreams to bed with England's final goal. They had done it! Harry threw himself on to Jordan – the superstar goalkeeper had saved the day.

The team were ecstatic to win a World Cup penalty shootout for only the second time in history. "To step up when it mattered and do what we did – I'm so proud of everyone involved," Harry told the press after the match. He was thrilled to shake off England's painful penalties past, as was Gareth. "We're trying to write our own history," the team's manager said proudly.

Penalty Shootouts

A football game goes to a penalty shootout in competitions where the game cannot end in a draw, and extra time has already expired. Each team takes turns shooting at the goal from the penalty mark, with the goal defended by only the opposing team's goalkeeper. Up to five different players from each team must take a shot, with the winners declared once one team has taken an unbeatable lead. Prior to the 2018 FIFA World Cup, England had only ever won one penalty shootout at a major tournament (the 1996 Euros). They have been knocked out of the World Cup three times through penalty shootouts.

Harry didn't manage to score in the next match against Sweden, but skilled shots from Dele Alli and Harry Maguire took England to a 2–0 finish.

Through to the Semi-finals

In the semi-finals, Harry and his team faced-off against Croatia. A record 20.7 million people tuned in to watch the match, the highest viewing figures for 2018 in the United Kingdom, and the noise inside the Luzhniki Stadium in Moscow was deafening. A goal from Kieran after five minutes of play gave England the advantage. Harry raced around the pitch, but struggled to get past the Croatian defences in order to get to the goal. At sixty-eight minutes, a pinpoint cross from Croatian Šime Vrsaljko's was met by teammate Ivan Perišić, who snuck the ball in at close range to equalize, and the game went to extra time. Though the England squad battled to the end, a shot from Mario Mandžukić ten minutes before the whistle dashed England's World Cup dreams. They were out of the competition.

Several of the England players collapsed on the pitch in despair. Gareth swept on to the field and pulled Harry into a hug, telling the striker just how proud he was. "We wanted to go all the way," Harry told an interviewer after the players had finally left the pitch. "It hurts. It's going to hurt for a little while."

By finishing fourth, England had gone further in the World Cup than they had for twenty-eight years. Once they got over their initial heartbreak, Harry and his teammates could hold their heads up high. Though England were denied their chance to raise the cup, Harry was awarded the Golden Boot for the highest goal tally in the tournament.

ONLY JUST
BEGINNING

A few weeks after Harry returned home, Kate gave birth to their second child. Vivienne "Vivi" Jane Kane was born on 6 August; Harry had her name and date of birth stitched on to his football boots beside Ivy's. Two weeks after she was born, he finally overcame his August goal drought, scoring in a match against Fulham.

By the end of December 2018, Harry was the second-highest scorer in the Premier League, with thirteen Premiership goals. A pair of special edition golden boots (gifted by Nike in honour of his World Cup performance) even topped the family's

Christmas tree! But on 13 January Harry suffered the first of two injuries that would keep him off the pitch for large chunks of the year. In a match against Sunderland, Harry tumbled to the ground and injured his leg again, forcing him out of the game for two months.

A Different Kind of Medal

On 28 March 2019, Harry was honoured for services to football in the Queen's 2019 New Year Honours list. Harry was a little nervous when he went to Buckingham Palace to collect his MBE, but Prince William, an Aston Villa fan, put him at ease, striking up a conversation about Harry's recent wins with England, as well as his charity work.

Injured Again

On 3 April 2019, Spurs played their first game at their brand-new home ground. The team marked the official opening of their £850 million stadium with a victory over Crystal Palace, cementing their place in the Premier League's top four. Tottenham Hotspur's stadium is the biggest club venue in London, with space for 62,062 fans, and the first stadium in the world to have a dividing retractable pitch, so it can double up as an NFL field.

The following week, Harry hurt his ankle again in a match against Manchester City. "Gutted to go off injured but every setback is a chance to come back stronger than ever," he tweeted. He was out for fifty-one days, but went along to as many of Tottenham's games as he could to cheer on the team as they battled it out in the Champions League. He also travelled to the United States for treatment, where he got to meet another of his heroes, Tom Brady. Harry was thrilled to meet Tom, and even got to hold his NFL trophy!

A Painful End

For the first time ever, Tottenham made it to the Champions League final. Mauricio decided to put Harry on the pitch for the all-important match, even though he hadn't played since April due to his injury. But it was Liverpool, not Spurs, who lifted the shining Champions League Cup after beating Tottenham 2–0. It was a painful way to end a season disrupted by injuries. Harry felt he could have performed better. But rather than wallow in regret, he was already looking to the future. "It makes you stronger, it makes you more determined," he said. "It builds the fire in the belly to get back there and, when we do hopefully get back there, prove a point."

Wedding Bells

On 19 June 2019, Harry and Kate got married. At the wedding of a footballer and a fitness instructor, sport was of course going to feature! The couple hosted their own sporting tournament called the Kaneland Games, which featured activities included golf – a favourite hobby of Harry's – bat and ball, Frisbee and limbo. The attendees even had matching sporty outfits.

The newlyweds set off on a relaxing honeymoon, enjoying lots of sea and sun, and getting ready for what would surely be another busy year.

Off the Pitch

Over the years, Harry has supported several charities, including Noah's Ark Hospice, a service providing support for children with life-limiting or life-threatening conditions. In 2019, Harry took part in a series of interviews encouraging young men to open up about their feelings. "Mental health is just as important as physical health," he told his Twitter followers. In one of the videos, Harry stands on a crossbar in a football field in Chingford as his voiceover states, "I am not afraid to ask for help, to tell my daughters I love them, to be myself. If that makes me different, I'll choose different every time." In August 2019, Harry launched a partnership between London's City Hall, the Metropolitan Police, and Premier League Kicks, an organization that gives young people access to free football sessions.

Looking Ahead

Before the 2019–20 season kicked off, Harry wowed the world with a wonder goal from the halfway line in a friendly match against Italian side Juventus. "What has he just done? Incredible!" the commentator cried in awe as the ball sailed high above the players to land in the opposition's goal. In his first Premier League match of the season, Harry made sure the fans were in no doubt that he was back on form, scoring two goals in the last ten minutes of the game. "I've come back ready to go, as the whole team has, and I feel sharp," he told the press. The striker was primed for another shot at a trophy – the Premier League, the Champions League and the Golden Boot were top of his list. Perhaps he could get all three.

A LASTING LEGACY

Harry Kane's first few years as a professional footballer have been outstanding. An exciting player to watch tear across the pitch, Harry somehow always seems to be in the right place at the right time. His superb ability isn't just a case of natural talent and good luck, but of hard work, courage and a refusal to give up when times are tough. Though his achievements so far have been incredible, Harry is sure that he can still be better, faster and stronger; that he can score more goals and lift a trophy. Harry has come a long way from the young lad Arsenal said wasn't athletic enough, but a hint of that stubborn schoolboy remains. It's the part of Harry that continues to hunt for an edge – from perfecting his technique to thinking carefully about his diet and taking the time for recovery, he will never stop fighting to improve his game.

Harry's made it clear that, all being well, he hopes for a long career in football. Given the dizzying heights he's already reached, it's exciting to imagine what he could go on to do over the next few years. And once his football career is over? "The desire to play in the NFL is real," he said in an interview. "It's something that in ten or twelve years I definitely want to try." Could Harry become a superstar in two sports? Only time will tell!

The Best is Yet to Come

In the entrance hall of Chingford Foundation School, Harry Kane's England Under-21s shirt now hangs beside David Beckham's Real Madrid shirt. For the students there, and for thousands of people around the world, Harry is an inspiration. He's an example of just how far a young footballer can go if they have the passion and drive.

Harry's teammates and managers have nothing but good things to say about him; he's the type of player who unites a club, rather than divides it.

"He's absolutely the role model you want in the dressing room."

GARETH SOUTHGATE

"Everyone talks about the goals but it's his work rate, humility and aggression that make Harry so incredible. He's so focused, full of hunger and constantly trying to improve."

ERIC DIER

"I believe he is the best player in the world in terms of mental strength, willpower and endeavour. He is completely focused on his football... He's the first to arrive and the last to leave."

MAURICIO POCHETTINO

Harry continues to celebrate his goals as if he is one of the fans in the stands. The thrill of getting the ball in the net is as strong as ever for the striker – after all, he's dreamed of scoring for Spurs and England since he was six years old. Harry is proof that working hard is more important than looking the part. His presence on the pitch is a reminder that the right attitude, buckets of enthusiasm and, above all, self-belief, can get you just about anywhere.

"I've got to where I am by working hard. But now I have to work even harder to stay here, because there's that next person who wants to take my position. That's my mindset: someone is always trying to be better than me, so I've got to make sure I work harder than anyone else."

HARRY KANE

Harry Kane Timeline

28 July 1993 Harry Kane is born.

30 June 1998 England go out of the World Cup in France after losing on penalties to Argentina.

1999 Manchester United win a unique treble of the Premier League title, FA Cup and European Cup.

2001 Harry Kane joins Arsenal's youth academy but leaves at the end of the season.

21 June 2002 England go out of the World Cup in Japan at the quarter-finals, losing 2–1 to Brazil.

2004	Harry joins Watford's youth academy. He is scouted by Spurs a few weeks later and joins their programme after successfully passing a trial.
2005	Harry meets David Beckham at the launch of the David Beckham Academy in Greenwich, London.
1 July 2006	England go out of the World Cup in Germany on penalties in their quarter-final against Portugal. Only one England player manages to score during the shootout.
28 July 2009	Harry signs a scholarship contract with Tottenham Hotspur.
27 October 2009	Harry is an unused substitute for Everton v. Tottenham in the Carling Cup. It is his first time on the bench for Spurs' first team.
February 2010	Harry plays for England in the Under-17s Algarve Tournament.

May 2010	Tottenham Hotspur break into the top four of the Premier League for the first time and qualify for the Champions League.
27 June 2010	England crash out of the World Cup in South Africa, losing 4–1 to Germany in the round of sixteen.
July 2010	Harry signs a five-year professional contract with Tottenham Hotspur.
7 January 2011	Harry goes on loan to Leyton Orient.
1 January 2012	Harry goes on loan to Millwall.
July 2012	Harry takes part in the Under-19s European Championships. Harry Redknapp steps down as manager at Spurs and is replaced by André Villas-Boas.
18 August 2012	Harry makes his Premier League debut, coming on in the eighty-fifth minute in a match against Newcastle.

31 August 2012	Harry goes on loan to Norwich City.
26 September 2012	Harry fractures a bone in his foot and returns to White Hart Lane to recover.
21 February 2013	Harry goes on loan to Leicester City.
May 2013	David Beckham retires from football.
June 2013	Harry takes part in the Under-20s World Cup.
December 2013	Spurs manager André Villas-Boas is replaced by Tim Sherwood.
7 April 2014	Harry gets his first start and first goal in a Premier League match against Sunderland.
May 2014	Tim Sherwood is replaced by Mauricio Pochettino as Spurs manager.
July 2014	England fail to qualify from the group stage at the World Cup in Brazil.

23 October 2014	Harry scores his first professional hat-trick against Asteras Tripolis.
January 2015	Jermain Defoe signs with Toronto FC and leaves Tottenham Hotspur. Harry scores a brace (two goals) against Chelsea. Harry wins Premier League Player of the Month for January.
7 February 2015	Harry scores twice against Arsenal in his first North London Derby. He goes on to win Premier League Player of the Month for February.
21 March 2015	Harry scores his first Premier League hat-trick against Leicester.
27 March 2015	Harry makes his England seniors debut, and marks it with a goal after seventy-nine seconds on the pitch.
26 December 2015	Harry breaks Teddy Sheringham's record of twenty-six goals in a calendar year for Spurs.

26 March 2016	Harry scores a spectacular goal against Germany in a friendly. He goes on to win Premier League Player of the Month for March.
May 2016	Harry wins the Premier League Golden Boot for 2015–16 with twenty-five goals. Leicester City win the Premier League for the first time in history.
June 2016	Harry plays for England at the Euros in France, but doesn't manage to score.
8 January 2017	Harry Kane and Kate Goodland's daughter, Ivy Jane Kane, is born.
February 2017	Harry wins Premier League Player of the Month for the fourth time.
14 May 2017	Tottenham play their final match at the White Hart Lane. Later that month, Harry wins the Premier League Golden Boot for the second time, with twenty-nine goals in 2016–17.

September 2017	Harry wins Premier League Player of the Month for the fifth time.
December 2017	Harry wins Premier League Player of the Month for the sixth time.
22 May 2018	Harry is named captain of England's World Cup team.
June–July 2018	Harry takes part in the 2018 World Cup, where England go out in the semi-final against Croatia. Harry wins the World Cup Golden Boot with six goals.
6 August 2018	Harry and Kate's second daughter, Vivienne "Vivi" Jane Kane, is born.
3 April 2019	Tottenham Hotspur play their first game in their new stadium.
19 June 2019	Harry and Kate get married.

Records and Honours

Harry has smashed countless records in his career. Here are seven of the best:

- Harry is one of only six players to win back-to-back Premier League Player of the Month awards (January and February 2015).
- Harry also holds the joint record for the most Premier League Player of the Month awards, with six wins. Steven Gerrard and Sergio Agüero have also won the award six times.
- On 26 December 2017, Harry Kane beat the record for most Premier League goals in a calendar year with thirty-nine goals across thirty-six games. Alan Shearer was the

previous top scorer with a tally of thirty-six goals across forty-two games in 1995.

- In 2017, Harry Kane scored fifty-six goals across all competitions – the most by any player in Europe, including a record six Premier League hat-tricks.
- On 4 February 2018, Harry joined "The 100 Club" with his one hundredth Premier League goal, against Liverpool, making him the second-fastest player to reach the milestone, behind Alan Shearer.
- Harry has been Tottenham Hotspur's top goalscorer for five consecutive seasons (from 2014–15 to 2018–19).
- On 1 January 2019, Harry Kane became the first Spurs player to have faced multiple opponents in the Premier League and scored against all of them.

Here are some of the awards and honours Harry has won over the years:

- Millwall Young Player of the Year: 2011–12
- PFA Young Player of the Year: 2014–15

- Premier League PFA Team of the Year: 2014–15, 2015–16, 2016–17, 2017–18
- Premier League Player of the Month: January 2015, February 2015, March 2016, February 2017, September 2017, December 2017
- Tottenham Hotspur Player of the Year: 2014–15
- Premier League Golden Boot: 2015–16, 2016–17
- PFA Fans' Player of the Year: 2016–17
- England Player of the Year Award: 2017, 2018
- FIFA World Cup Golden Boot: 2018
- Member of the Order of the British Empire (MBE): 2019

Harry's Heroes

Meet three football legends who inspired Harry to follow his dreams!

Teddy Sheringham

Position: Striker

Clubs: Millwall, Nottingham Forest, Tottenham Hotspur, Manchester United, Portsmouth, West Ham

---

Career highlight: Winning three trophies in a single season with Manchester United. In 1998–99, Manchester United won the Premier League, FA Cup and the Champions League

---

Spectacular stat: Teddy scored a total of 125 goals for Tottenham and is their tenth-highest goalscorer of all time

---

Wise words: "To me, football means a passion in life. It's all I ever wanted to do as a kid. I loved getting better as I got older and then playing with some of the best players in the world."

David Beckham

Position: Midfielder

Clubs: Manchester United, Preston North End, Real Madrid, Milan, LA Galaxy, Paris Saint-Germain

---

Epic moment: Scoring an equaliser in the last two minutes of a game against Greece to take England to the World Cup finals in 2002

Spectacular stat: David was the first British footballer to play a hundred Champions League fixtures

---

Wise words: "The only time you run out of chances is when you stop taking them."

Jermain Defoe

Position: Striker

Clubs: West Ham, Bournemouth, Tottenham Hotspur, Portsmouth, Toronto FC, Sunderland, Rangers

---

Epic moment: Scoring against Slovenia in the 2010 World Cup, helping England to qualify for the round of sixteen

---

Spectacular stat: He is the eighth-highest goalscorer in Premier League history, and the sixth-highest goalscorer for Spurs, netting 143 times before he left the club in 2013

Wise words: "When you get up in the morning and know you're doing something you love, feel fit and look after yourself, it's just a great thing to do."

Harry's Clubs

Tottenham Hotspur

Club name: Tottenham Hotspur Football Club
Nickname: The Lilywhites
Short name: Spurs
Founded: 1882 (as Hotspur)
Current manager: Mauricio Pochettino
Current league: Premier League
Crest: A cockerel standing on a football, with a Latin motto *Audere Est Facere*, which means "To Dare Is to Do"

Spurs Song

Spurs fans have several chants, here's one of their favourites:

Oh, when the Spurs
Go marching in,
Oh, when the Spurs go marching in,
I wanna be in that number,
When the Spurs go marching in...

Leyton Orient

Club name: Leyton Orient Football Club
Nicknames: The Os, Orient
Founded: 1881
Current manager: Carl Fletcher
Current league: League Two
Crest: Two wyverns (dragon-like guardians of the River Thames) facing each other over a football

Millwall

Club name: Millwall Football Club

Nicknames: The Lions
Founded: 1885 (as Millwall Rovers)
Current manager: Gary Rowett
Current league: Championship
Crest: A roaring blue lion

Leicester City

Club name: Leicester City Football Club
Nicknames: The Foxes
Founded: 1884 (as Leicester Fosse FC)
Current manager: Brendan Rodgers
Current league: Premier League
Crest: A fox's head overlaid on a five-petalled flower

Norwich City

Club name: Norwich City Football Club
Nickname: The Canaries
Founded: 1902
Current manager: Daniel Farke
Current league: Premier League
Crest: A canary perched on a football, with elements of Norwich's coat of arms in the top-left corner

Harry's Favourite Goals

Harry's got the ball in the back of the net over 130 times in the Premier League, and over twenty times for England – that's a lot of top goals to choose from! But a few fantastic finishes stand out from the rest.

First Goal in the Premier League

When: 7 April 2014
Playing: Sunderland
How it happened: Christian Eriksen curled a cross into the six-yard box and Harry tapped in the ball

Winning Goal in the North London Derby

When: 7 February 2015
Playing: Arsenal

How it happened: Having already scored once at fifty-six minutes, Harry took his team to victory with a header from the centre of the box to the top-left corner after an assist by Nabil Bentaleb

First Goal for England

When: 27 March 2015
Playing: Lithuania
How it happened: After just seventy-nine seconds on the pitch, Harry headed in a cross from Raheem Sterling

First Goal in the World Cup

When: 18 June 2018
Playing: Tunisia
How it happened: John Stones' header from Ashley Young's corner was saved by the goalkeeper, but Harry was ready to tap it in from three yards out

Harry's Golden Rules of Goalscoring

Pay attention to these top tips and you too could become a fantastic finisher just like Harry.

Do What You're Good At

"You can't go on to the pitch trying to play like anyone else. You have to play your own game and do what you know you're good at. Playing to your strengths is the most important thing."

Shoot Low and Hard

"When you get a clear sight of goal, aim low and hard across the goalkeeper. These are the most difficult shots to save."

Shoot Early

"I like to get my shots away early . . . shooting early can catch the goalkeeper off-guard."

If It Doesn't Go In, Try Again

"It's very important for a striker to score rebounds. A goal's a goal."

Be Where You Need to Be

"It [is] all about being in the right place at the right time – that's down to movement, training and experience – reading where the ball is going to drop and getting there before the defender does."

Believe In Yourself

"If you don't believe in yourself, not many others will. Work hard and believe in yourself, and I think you'll go as far as your body will take you."

If you loved reading about Harry Kane, why not read about Raheem Sterling next?

If you loved reading about **Harry Kane**, why not read about **Raheem Sterling** next?

KINGSTON, JAMAICA, 1996

Raheem was just two years old, and he had only one parent left.

At the time his dad died, Raheem and his family were living in Kingston, the capital of Jamaica, in an area called Maverley. He was born there, six years after his sister, and it was the kind of place where everyone knew everyone, and where the children always played outside. When there was a storm, the rain would decorate the grey streets, and the children would rush laughing through the puddles; and because the rain was so warm, running in it felt like taking a shower.

People in Raheem's neighbourhood didn't have very much. They had to work hard just so there was enough for everyone. All they really had was their friends and their siblings and their mums and their dads, and some of them didn't even have that.

No one knew exactly what happened to Raheem's dad, but what they did know was that one day some people got very angry with him and went looking for him with their guns. When they found him, they didn't talk, they fired, and that's how they took Raheem's dad away.

It was one of the hardest times in Raheem's life, and it was about to get even harder. Soon his mum had to leave too. She couldn't find a job that paid well enough in Jamaica, so she went to the UK to study there and hopefully earn enough to support her children. Raheem was too young to understand why she had to go. All he knew was that he used to have two parents, and now it felt like he had none.

Surrounded By Love

But even though he had lost his dad forever and his mum had gone far away, Raheem was still surrounded by love. He and his sister went to live with their grandmother.

If he was good Raheem's grandmother would let him go and buy ice cream from the local shop. So many small towns in Jamaica have a shop like that, where it feels like you can buy anything. You normally find them on the corner of a street, and they look very small from the outside, but once you walk inside it's like being in a cave. You just have to tell the shopkeeper what you want, and he'll disappear into a little room at the back for a few seconds before coming out with whatever you asked for. You could ask him for some batteries, a toothbrush, a kettle, even a chicken – just give him a few minutes, and he would return with it in his hands.

That was how Raheem's life started: with some very sad times, but some very happy ones too. Ice cream, running through the rain – and, of course, lots of busy days playing football with his friends. But for him to have a life more exciting than he could imagine, he would have to get on a plane.

DOES THIS COUNTRY HAVE A SUN?

When Raheem was five years old, he and his sister moved to his new home – to the city of London, the capital of England. They had gone there to be with their mum, but they soon found that London was very, very different from Jamaica. The buildings were taller and the traffic was louder and the crowds were bigger and, maybe most of all, the weather was colder. Some days he would look up at the sky and ask himself, "Does this country even have a sun?"

Raheem lived in a part of London called Wembley. There were so many people there from all over the world, which meant that at his new school Raheem met children from lots of countries he hadn't heard of before. There were people there from England and India and Sri Lanka and Kenya and Pakistan and Somalia and Ireland and Poland and from Jamaica, just like Raheem. If you walked down the main street and listened carefully, you could hear a new language. If you stopped next to the open door of each restaurant, you could smell a new type of food.

When people met Raheem in his new home they noticed that he didn't talk very much, and they thought he was shy. But he wasn't – he was just getting to know them, working out if he could trust them. When he got to know you well, he talked a lot more.

In View of Greatness

There were plenty of good things about Wembley but there were two that Raheem loved more than anything else. The first thing was that this was the home of Wembley Stadium, the most famous football ground in the world. You could see the stadium from all over the area, and when England were playing, crowds filled the local pubs and people sang songs about their team late into the night, even if they didn't win.

The second thing, of course, was that he was with his mum again. Now he was here, he understood why she had left Jamaica. There were more chances to study in England, and to earn good money. But how he had missed her! He had missed everything about her – the way she laughed and the way she cooked and even the way she said "Raheem!" when she was telling him to stop dashing around the house, because he often knocked things over. Yes – he even missed being told off. And now that his family was back together, now he and his mum and his sister were all sleeping under the same roof, which was all that mattered. When he remembered this, he felt brave enough to do anything.

Wembley Stadium

The Wembley Stadium Raheem loved as a child was knocked down in 2002. A new stadium was built in 2007. It can seat 90,000 people for football matches and is the largest stadium in the UK.

Coming soon!

Be inspired by more Football Legends.

Two new titles available September 2020